D1271603

by Amber Bullis

FAMOUS GHOST STORIES OF AFRICA

HAUNTED WORLD

EDGE BOOKS

CAPSTONE PRESS
a capstone imprint

Edge Books are published by Capstone Press,
1710 Roe Crest Drive, North Mankato, Minnesota 56003
www.mycapstone.com

Library of Congress Cataloging-in-Publication Data
Library of Congress Cataloging-in-Publication Data is available on the Library
of Congress website.
ISBN: 978-1-5435-2594-6 (hardcover)
ISBN: 978-1-5435-2598-4 (paperback)
ISBN: 978-1-5435-2602-8 (eBook PDF)

Editorial Credits
Carrie Braulick Sheely, editor; Kyle Grenz, designer; Svetlana Zhurkin,
media researcher; Kathy McColley, production specialist

Photo Credits
Alamy: Antony Souter, 7, davidwallphoto, 12, Radius Images, 26–27, Víctor
Suárez, 17; Bridgeman Images: Private Collection/Portrait Miniature of Lady
Anne Barnard (w/c on ivory in gilt-metal frame), Mee, Anne (Mrs. Joseph)
(c. 1760-1851)/Photo © Philip Mould Ltd, London, 13; Dreamstime: Kaido
Rummel, cover (back), Lesapi, 10; iStockphoto: Goddard_Photography, 9;
Library of Congress, 23 (bottom); Newscom: Dumont Bildar/picture-alliance/
Arthur F. Selbach, 19, Heritage Images/Werner Forman Archive/Euan Wingfield,
28; Shutterstock: Anton Belo, 23 (top), Armita (map), 5, 8, 10, 14, 16, 18, 20,
22, 24, 26, 29, Brian Kinney, 24, David Steele, 4, Daxiao Productions, cover
(front), Elenarts, 15, HandmadePictures, 5, michaeljung, 18, Peter Titmuss, 11,
PrakichTreetasayuth, 8, Sopotnicki, 20–21, Waj, 25

Design Elements by Shutterstock

Printed and bound in the USA.
122018   000057

TABLE OF CONTENTS

Scary Ghost Stories of Africa

What was the last ghost story you heard? Maybe it involved a local haunted cemetery or hotel. People tell similar spooky tales all over the world. Some of these stories come from Africa. Does a ghostly woman join party guests at a historic castle in South Africa? Do ancient Egyptian kings haunt their burial places? Decide for yourself as you explore some of Africa's most haunted places.

haunted—having mysterious events happen often, possibly due to visits from ghosts

Tokai Manor House In Cape Town, South Africa, is said to be haunted by a ghostly horse and rider.

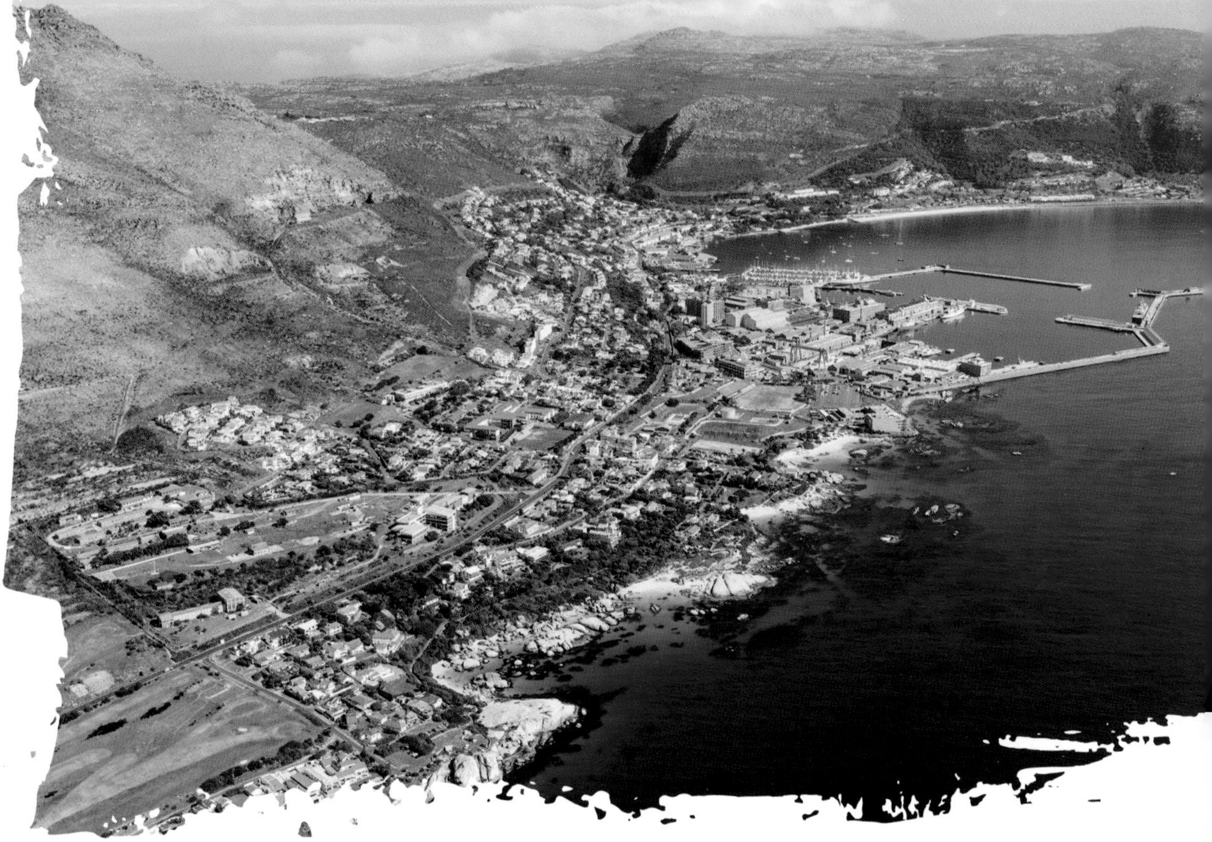

Simon's Town

LOCATION: CAPE TOWN, SOUTH AFRICA

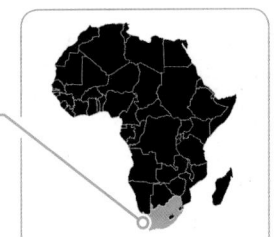

For more than 200 years, Simon's Town has been a Navy base for the South African Navy. Today the base is known not only for its military importance but also for its ghost stories. Spooky stories about Simon's Town include ghosts who bang on doors and knock paintings from walls. Some people have felt unexplained chilly air in hallways. In one building witnesses have reported the ghosts of a nurse and an old man who sits on a toilet.

Magistrates used a building called The Residency in the early 1800s. The Residency was home to cells where guards chained and punished prisoners. Today locals say the ghosts of former prisoners haunt The Residency. Some visitors claim to have seen ghost prisoners in a cell. Unexplained chilly winds blast through the rooms and cell doors bang shut on their own. Some people believe one of the ghosts is a seaman who faced a gruesome death. A guard's wife who treated prisoners poorly is also said to haunt the building.

In 1982 The Residency became the Simon's Town Museum. Workers at the museum have reported seeing a ghost in old-fashioned clothes. They say she turns off lights, moves objects around, and makes noises in empty rooms. Workers began to call her the "Grey Lady" because she is often seen wearing a gray dress. One story says she is the ghost of a servant who lived at The Residency in the 1700s. She was in love with a sailor but was not allowed to see him. Another story says she is the ghost of a teenage girl who once lived at The Residency.

magistrate—a government official who makes and enforces laws

Soweto Ghost Child

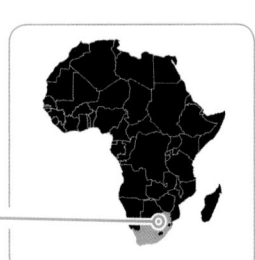

LOCATION: JOHANNESBURG, SOUTH AFRICA

On June 16, 1976, schoolchildren protested in the Soweto neighborhood in Johannesburg, South Africa. During the protests, 13-year-old Hector Pieterson was shot by police. A reporter took his picture as the injured boy was carried away. Hector died from his wounds. A South African newspaper published the picture, and other newspapers around the world soon did too. It was one of the most important moments in the struggle against apartheid in South Africa. It showed the world what was happening there. It led to continued protests against apartheid, which would later be known as the Soweto Uprising.

Soweto neighborhood of Johannesburg

apartheid—a former policy of racial segregation and discrimination in South Africa

Today there is a memorial to Hector and others who died in the uprising near where he was shot. At the foot of the hill after sunset, people claim to see Hector. He has his fist raised in a black power salute. Some people say the faint sound of gunfire can also be heard.

FACT

South Africa made June 16 a holiday. People remember the 1976 protest on this day.

The Castle of Good Hope

LOCATION: CAPE TOWN, SOUTH AFRICA

The Dutch East India Company built the Castle of Good Hope between 1666 and 1679. The trading company wanted the fort to provide protection in case the settlement was attacked. The castle is the oldest building still used today in South Africa. Some believe it's also the most haunted. In the late 1600s, locals used the Castle of Good Hope for fancy balls, ceremonies, and other events. But the castle also had a dark side. An underground prison and torture chamber called the "dark hole" was deep within its concrete walls. Officials imprisoned, tortured, and executed people held in the dark hole. Could the castle's bloody past explain some of its paranormal events?

execute—to put to death
paranormal—having to do with an event that has no scientific explanation

Visitors have reported many ghosts at the castle. The ghost of an angry man matches the description of a cruel governor. The governor once sentenced seven prisoners to death. He mysteriously died the same day he sentenced the prisoners. A ghostly black dog is said to jump at visitors and then disappear. Visitors have also seen a ghostly man with no legs.

Some ghosts at the Castle of Good Hope might even be able
to make physical contact with the living. A worker once stayed
overnight at the castle because he didn't have a ride home. He
reported feeling an unexplained heaviness on his chest during the
night. He also felt like his body was tied up and that he couldn't
move. After struggling free, he ran out of the room, terrified.

One of the most famous ghosts of the castle is said to be of Lady Anne Barnard. Lady Anne moved with her husband, Andrew Barnard, to the Castle of Good Hope in 1797. She hosted grand parties there. Castle guards have reported seeing Lady Anne's ghost in a beautiful gown joining guests at ballroom parties. A painting of peacocks that Lady Anne hung is still on a wall in her former drawing room. It is said that anyone who moves it will die. Castle workers now keep it covered just to be safe.

Lady Anne Barnard

The Flying Dutchman

LOCATION: SEA SURROUNDING THE CAPE OF GOOD HOPE, SOUTH AFRICA

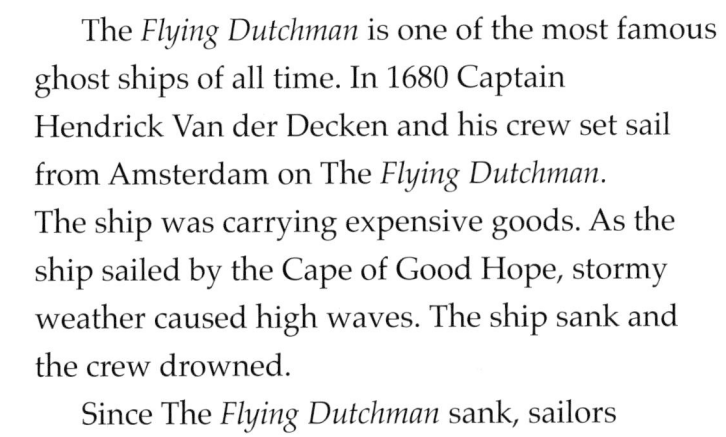

The *Flying Dutchman* is one of the most famous ghost ships of all time. In 1680 Captain Hendrick Van der Decken and his crew set sail from Amsterdam on The *Flying Dutchman*. The ship was carrying expensive goods. As the ship sailed by the Cape of Good Hope, stormy weather caused high waves. The ship sank and the crew drowned.

Since The *Flying Dutchman* sank, sailors have reported seeing the ghost ship. Many of these sightings happen during bad weather. Some stories say The *Flying Dutchman* approached other ships until they almost collided before the ghost ship disappeared. Other stories say the ghost ship sent an eerie glow into the sky or appeared in the middle of a red flame. The most famous person to see the ghost ship is said to be King George V of England. Before becoming king, he served in the Royal Navy. In 1881 he was aboard the ship *Bacchante*. He wrote about the crew's ghostly encounter with The *Flying Dutchman* in his diary.

Sailors aren't the only ones who say The *Flying Dutchman* still haunts the waters around the cape. On at least two separate occasions, crowds at a beach saw The *Flying Dutchman*. The ghost ship is said to have disappeared after almost colliding with the shore.

FACT

It's said that a sailor who sees *The Flying Dutchman* will die shortly afterward.

Sarpan Island

LOCATION: DAKAR, SENEGAL

Just off the coast of Dakar, Senegal, is tiny Sarpan Island. It's one of the rocky islands of the Iles de Madeleine and is part of a national park. According to legend, it is also home to a magical spirit called a genie, or djinn.

Local fishers believe the genie protects them. But if someone makes the genie angry, the genie will keep that person from catching any fish. Some even say it will crash the offender's boat on the rocks of the island. According to a guide, the captain of a Spanish tuna boat saw a light on the island in 2013. The boat ran aground. However, no one lives on the island and there are no lights.

The genie does not want anyone living on the island. In the 1700s a man named Lacombe tried to build a house there out of island rock. According to legend, the spirit kept destroying the house. He later left the island with the house unfinished. Visitors can still see the ruins today.

FACT

Sarpan Island is known for its small baobab trees and the seabirds that nest there.

Port Elizabeth Public Library

LOCATION: PORT ELIZABETH, SOUTH AFRICA

Some call the Port Elizabeth Public Library the most beautiful building in South Africa. In 1902 builders constructed the library with gorgeous archways, stained-glass windows, spiral staircases, and a large glass dome. Yet its impressive appearance may be hiding some spooky secrets.

Locals say the library has been home to at least two ghosts. Before the library's construction, a different building stood on the library grounds. In 1896 a fire destroyed it. When firefighters tried to put out the fire, a large piece of stone fell off the building and killed a police officer. Locals put up a stone to remember the policeman. As construction of the new library began, workers moved the stone to the garden. But the police officer's ghost might not have been happy about the new location of his remembrance stone. People say he haunted room 700 of the library until workers moved the stone back to its original location.

People believe a former library caretaker also haunts the building. Robert Thomas worked at the library for 31 years. Since his death in 1943, workers say doors mysteriously open and shut and books move or fall when no one is around. Could Thomas' devotion to the library have kept him there even after death?

Menengai Crater

LOCATION: NAKURU, KENYA

The mysterious Menengai Crater is located about 100 miles (160 kilometers) from Nairobi, Kenya. It's the crater of a volcano that erupted thousands of years ago. Hot vents in some parts of the crater still give off steam today.

The name *Menengai* seems to have come from the Maasai culture. It means "place of the dead." In the 1800s two groups of Maasai fought each other at the crater. According to legend, the winners threw the losers into the crater.

FACT

The Menengai Crater is the second largest volcanic crater in the world.

Locals sometimes call it "Devil's Place," for the supernatural beings said to live there. These beings are even said to farm on the crater floor. The crops would be planted, grown, and harvested within a day. Some people think the spirits trick visitors and hunters into getting lost. Sometimes they disappear. Other times they are found wandering after several days. When asked, they can't seem to explain how they got lost.

supernatural—something that cannot be given an ordinary explanation

Valley of the Kings

LOCATION: LUXOR, EGYPT

Ancient Egyptians used the Valley of the Kings as a burial site from about 1539 to 1075 BC. Egyptians buried **pharaohs** and other royal leaders in the tombs. They **mummified** the bodies to preserve them for the **afterlife**. With all the dead bodies there, it may not be surprising that the site has been the focus of some creepy ghost stories.

The valley is one of Egypt's major tourist sites. Some visitors have reported unexplained feelings of being watched. Others report hearing ghostly screams and mysterious footsteps. The most common ghost story tells of a pharaoh wearing a golden headdress. He haunts the valley on a chariot pulled by black ghost horses.

Visitors to the valley also have reported seeing the ghost of the pharaoh Akhenaten. Egyptian priests are said to have put a curse on him because he banned worship of the Egyptian gods. The curse forced him to wander the valley forever. Could the curse have worked?

pharaoh—a king of ancient Egypt

mummify—to preserve a body with special salts and cloth to make it last for a very long time; the preserved bodies are called mummies

afterlife—the life that some people believe begins when a person dies

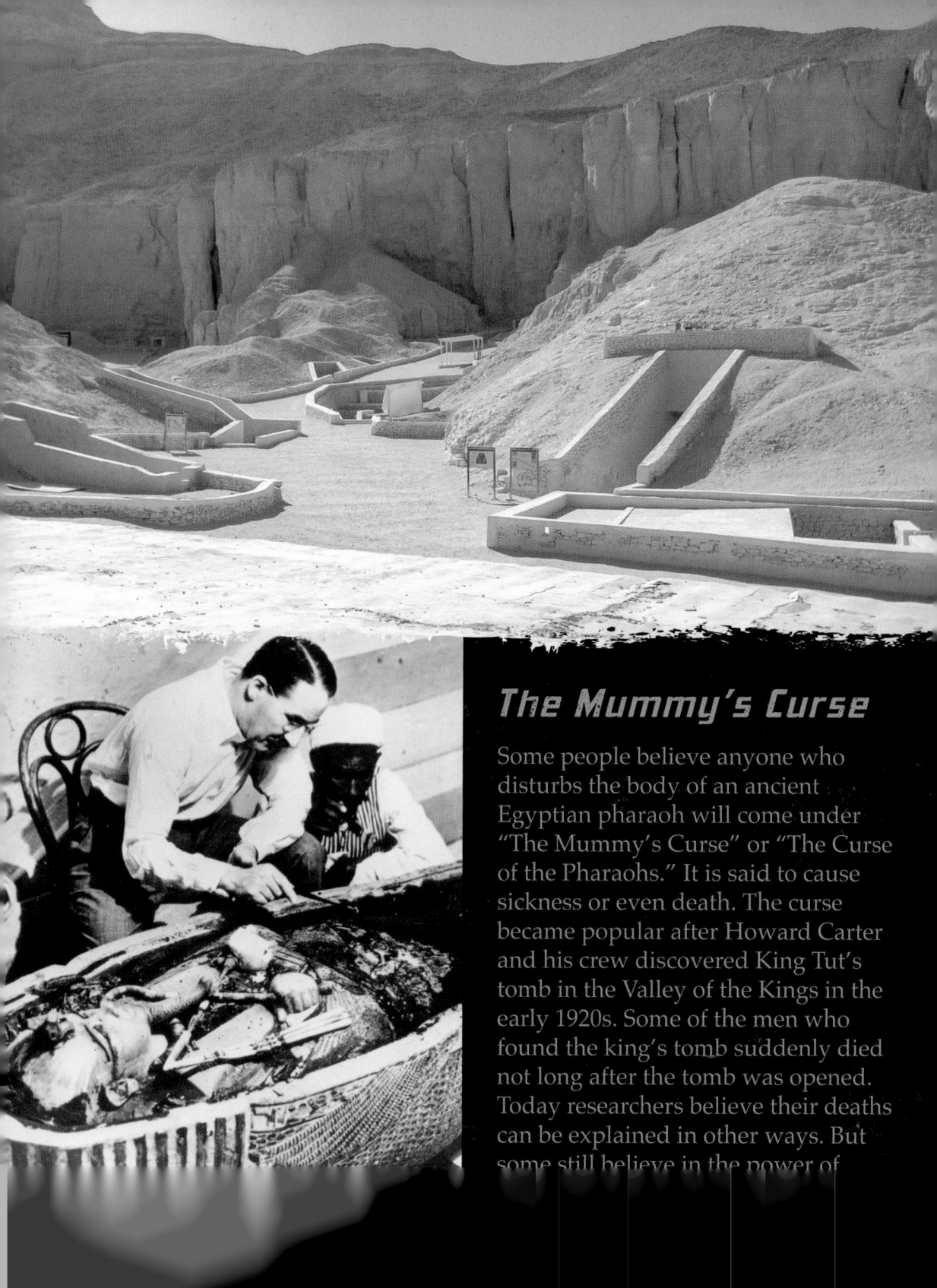

The Mummy's Curse

Some people believe anyone who disturbs the body of an ancient Egyptian pharaoh will come under "The Mummy's Curse" or "The Curse of the Pharaohs." It is said to cause sickness or even death. The curse became popular after Howard Carter and his crew discovered King Tut's tomb in the Valley of the Kings in the early 1920s. Some of the men who found the king's tomb suddenly died not long after the tomb was opened. Today researchers believe their deaths can be explained in other ways. But some still believe in the power of

The Pyramids of Giza

LOCATION: GIZA, EGYPT

Egyptians used the Pyramids of Giza as tombs for pharaohs before the Valley of the Kings. They built the Pyramids of Giza between about 2575 and 2465 BC. Three pyramids make up the landmark. Pharaoh Khufu ordered the building of the biggest pyramid, known as the Great Pyramid. Ancient Egyptians built the second pyramid that includes the Sphinx for pharaoh Khafre. The Sphinx is a statue with the body of a lion and the head of a pharaoh. Pharaoh Menkaure ordered the third and smallest pyramid.

People reported ghosts at the Pyramids of Giza as early as 1900. Witnesses have reported seeing the ghost of a British soldier with fiery eyes. The soldier is said to have fallen from one of the pyramids in 1882. Another ghost haunting the area is said to be of a worker who died running machinery nearby.

Dr. Paul Brunton spent the night in the Great Pyramid in the 1930s. He said he felt his entire body go numb and cold. He saw ghostly figures move across the room. One raised its hands and came at him in a threatening way. Does something paranormal go on at night in the pyramids? Few people get permission to stay there overnight, so perhaps we'll never know.

FACT

Archaeologists are still unsure how ancient Egyptians built the massive pyramids at Giza. Scientists say the pharaohs needed between 20,000 and 30,000 workers to build the Great Pyramid. These workers had to transport about 2.3 million stone blocks that each weighed 2.5 to 15 tons!

Kaf Ajnoun

LOCATION: NEAR GHAT, LIBYA

A natural rock formation in Libya called Kaf Ajnoun has many names, and most of them relate to ghosts. It is known as the Mountain of Ghosts, the Devil's Hill, and the Fortress of Ghosts. The local Tuareg people believe spirits live there. Many locals are so scared of the spirits that they will not travel near it.

The Tuaregs share stories of wicked spirits that gather on the mountain and will scare anyone who tries to climb it. In the 1500s a traveler wrote that evil spirits haunted the mountain. He said spirits confused travelers so they couldn't find their way home. Explorers who have dared to go there have often encountered difficulties. Two different explorers in the mid-1800s got lost on the mountain and nearly died. One was the famous explorer Heinrich Barth. He ran out of water and survived by drinking his own blood.

Some locals believe the ghosts that live on the formation can even enter the bodies of animals and people. One story tells of evil spirits entering wasps to warn climbers to stay off the mountain. French travelers who wanted to hike the mountain raced back to their vehicle after a swarm of wasps attacked them, leaving their faces full of painful stings. They never climbed the mountain. In 2004 explorer Kira Salak climbed the mountain. At first, she believed she made it home safe. But months later, she said evil ghosts entered her body. Could the local stories be true? Explorers may want to stay far away from Kaf Ajnoun so they don't find out.

FACT

One man said he watched an army of terrifying ghosts marching on the mountain before they suddenly disappeared.

Camels help Tuaregs travel around the hot African deserts.

Haunted Locations of Africa

1. Simon's Town, South Africa
2. Soweto Ghost Child, Johannesburg, South Africa
3. The Castle of Good Hope, Cape Town, South Africa
4. *The Flying Dutchman*, seas near Cape of Good Hope
5. Sarpan Island, Dakar, Senegal
6. Port Elizabeth Library, Port Elizabeth, South Africa
7. Menengai Crater, Nakuru, Kenya
8. Valley of the Kings, Luxor, Egypt
9. The Pyramids of Giza, Giza, Egypt
10. Kaf Ajnoun, near Ghat, Libya
11. Rudd House, Kimberley, South Africa
12. Kempton Park Hospital, Kempton Park, South Africa

GLOSSARY

afterlife (AF-tur-life)—the life that some people believe begins after a person dies

apartheid (uh-PAR-tayt)—a former policy of racial segregation and discrimination in South Africa

execute (EK-si-kyoot)—to put to death

haunted (HAWNT-id)—having mysterious events happen often, possibly due to visits from ghosts

legend (LEJ-uhnd)—a story passed down through the years that may not be completely true

magistrate (MA-juh-strayt)—a government official who makes and enforces laws

mummify (MUH-mih-fy)—to preserve a body with special salts and cloth to make it last for a very long time; the preserved bodies are called mummies

paranormal (pair-uh-NOR-muhl)—having to do with an event that has no scientific explanation

pharaoh (FAIR-oh)—a king of ancient Egypt

supernatural (soo-pur-NACH-ur-uhl)—something that cannot be given an ordinary explanation

READ MORE

Doeden, Matt. *The Queen Mary: A Chilling Interactive Adventure.* You Choose: Haunted Places. North Mankato, Minn.: Capstone Press, 2017.

Peterson, Megan Cooley. *Haunted Hotels Around the World.* It's Haunted! North Mankato, Minn.: Capstone Press, 2017.

Ramsey, Grace. *Haunted Houses.* Yikes! It's Haunted. Vero Beach, Fla.: Rourke Educational Media, 2016.

INTERNET SITES

Use FactHound to find Internet sites related to this book.

Visit *www.facthound.com*

Just type in 9781543525946 and go.

 **Super-cool stuff!** Check out projects, games and lots more at **www.capstonekids.com**

INDEX